ST GEOR
& THE ENGLISH S

PETER BRIMACOMBE

The word 'saint' derives from the Latin *sanctus*, essentially meaning 'holy one'. Saints have existed since biblical times, the cult originating in the beliefs and customs of Jewry and early Christianity. The earliest Christian saints were martyrs, a word deriving from the Greek for witness, the apostles being witnesses to the resurrection of Christ. The term then came to signify those prepared to sacrifice their lives in pursuit of their faith.

The veneration of saints has existed since the 2nd century, the first English martyr being Alban, a citizen of Verulamium, modern day St Albans, who was beheaded by the Romans for sheltering a Christian priest *c.*AD 304, around the time that St George was, according to legend, martyred in a far away land.

Initially, saints were created by popular acclaim, sometimes very localized, revered perhaps for their piety, missionary zeal, fortitude, wisdom or ability to perform miracles. In the late 12th century, Pope Alexander III decreed that only the papacy could create saints, a tradition maintained ever since, the Anglican church choosing not to perpetuate canonization after breaking with Rome. Today, though, the 'communion of saints' remains at the heart of both churches' liturgy. Saints continue to capture our imagination, to inspire and give comfort in an increasingly materialistic and turbulent world.

St George, the Mystery Man

The origins of England's most famous saint are shrouded in mystery. Indeed, so little is known about George that doubts have been expressed over his very existence. It is thought that he was a soldier beheaded *c.*AD 304 at Lydda in Palestine during Diocletian's persecution of the Christians. King Arthur is said to have had the image of St George on his banners in the 6th century and legend also has it that the saint appeared in a vision before the Christian army at Antioch in Syria during the First Crusade in 1098. Richard the Lionheart placed his army under St George's protection during the Third Crusade, their fluttering battle flags displaying the now familiar red cross on a white background. Returning crusaders popularized St George throughout medieval England.

George's status was further enhanced in the 14th century when Edward III founded the Order of the Garter at Windsor Castle with St George as its patron, at the same time rededicating the castle's chapel, formerly dedicated to St Edward the Confessor, to include the saint.

Gradually, the more charismatic George replaced the pious Edward as the nation's patron saint. In 1415, he was immortalized by Henry V's archers at the Battle of Agincourt and later by Edward IV's new chapel at Windsor, built next to its predecessor Critics question George's right to be patron saint as he is not English. Yet neither was St Patrick Irish or St Andrew born in Scotland.

LEFT: This boss in the nave of Exeter Cathedral depicts St George and the Dragon. A boss is a knob, often richly carved, at the intersection of the arches which support a rib vault.

ABOVE: St George's statue on the west front of Salisbury Cathedral. In contrast with England's patron saint, St Petroc, patron saint of Cornwall, was said to have been kind to dragons.

Hurrah! Hurrah! St George and Merrie England!'

The battle cry of Henry V's archers at Agincourt

The story of St George and the dragon is allegorical, a symbolic ·presentation of good overcoming evil. In the Bible, the book of evelation depicts Satan as a dragon opposed by the Archangel lichael, God's commander of the Heavenly Host. The legend linking t George to the dragon only became widespread in England well fter he was recognized as a saint. Today he remains the patron saint f England, his cross on the country's national flag proudly flying hroughout the kingdom, especially on 23 April, St George's Day, ie day on which he is thought to have been executed.

BOVE: Carlo Marochetti's imposing statue of Richard the Lionheart outside the Palace of /estminster, London. It was first displayed at the Great Exhibition of 1851.

ABOVE: A wooden carving of St George and the dragon, discovered in the choir canopies of St George's Chapel, Windsor, in the 1980s.

St George and the Dragon

This tale derives from the Golden Legend, written in the 13th century, involving Sabra, a king's daughter, about to be sacrificed to appease a ferocious dragon terrorizing the kingdom. St George rescued her from certain death by thrusting his lance into the dragon's mouth, killing it instantly. The grateful king and hordes of his subjects became Christians.

England's Highest Order of Chivalry

The Most Noble Order of the Garter, England's highest order of chivalry, was founded by Edward III in 1348, both its name and motto supposedly stemming from an incident at a court ball celebrating the capture of Calais. The garter of the pretty young Countess of Salisbury, known as 'the fair maid of Kent', fell to the ground. The king is said to have bent down and, with a flourish, tied it around his left knee. The murmur that ran around the room was quickly silenced by the king's stentorian '*Honi soit qui mal y pense*' (Shame on him who thinks this evil). It makes a good story.

The annual ceremony of the Order usually takes place in June, when the sovereign, accompanied by the Prince of Wales and 24 Knights Companion, parades through the middle and lower wards of Windsor Castle to St George's Chapel, attended by heralds and the Queen's Body Guard. Lining the route are troops from the Household Cavalry and the Guards. The formal investiture of new Knights of the Garter takes place at the service. All participants are in full ceremonial dress, this historic event representing a unique example of the nation's rich pageantry.

ABOVE: HM The Queen wearing the robes of the Order with the Garter Star and St George's Cross at the annual Order of the Garter ceremony.

ABOVE: Henry VIII surrounded by his Knights of the Garter. He brutally swept aside anyone who, like Sir Thomas More, declined to obey his will.

LEFT: The choir and chancel of St George's Chapel, Windsor. Banners of the Knights of the Garter hang beneath the magnificent fan-vaulted ceiling. The chapel comes directly under the jurisdiction of the sovereign, rather than a bishop.

St George's Chapel was founded in 1475 to be the chapel of the Order of the Garter, whose colourful banners now hang from the walls of the choir. Edward was the first of ten monarchs to be buried in the chapel, the most recent being George VI, Queen Elizabeth II's father.

Completed in 1528, it was built in the Perpendicular style, that final glorious period of Gothic architecture when new technology enabled artistry of the highest order – a delicate stone structure with slender, soaring columns, exquisitely intricate fan-vaulted ceiling and enormous stained-glass windows. The west window, reputedly England's third largest, contains medieval figures of kings, popes and saints including St Alban and St Dunstan, two early English saints. A beautifully carved wooden statue of St George slaying the dragon can be found on a ledge outside the Oliver King Chapel (south transept) with another statue of the saint on the tomb of the Duke of Clarence in the Albert Memorial Chapel, a huge monument designed by Sir Alfred Gilbert, the creator of 'Eros' in Piccadilly. This is just some of the superb craftsmanship to be seen in one of the nation's greatest architectural wonders.

A Light in the Dark

By AD 410 the Romans were departing British shores. During the Dark Ages which followed, the Christian candle flickered solely in the Celtic West, a glimmer of hope in an otherwise barbaric land. When Christianity returned, it was to Lindisfarne, otherwise known as Holy Island, off the wild Northumbrian coast, and also to Cornwall, accounting for the huge number of early Christian saints to be found in that part of the West Country. Among them were St Ia who, legend has it, floated over the sea to Cornwall on a leaf; St Minver, said to be one of St Brychan's 24 children; and St Enodoc, whose church on the north Cornish coast is where Sir John Betjeman is buried. St Neot is thought to have been a monk at Glastonbury who became a hermit on Bodmin Moor. King Alfred reputedly visited him in order to seek the saint's advice, the story of his burning the cakes deriving from an account of St Neot's life.

Pope Gregory, aware of the revival of Christianity in England and wishing to establish his authority there, dispatched Augustine on a mission to convert heathen southern England in 596. The future saint became the first Archbishop of Canterbury, founding the cathedral there shortly after his arrival. However, his unfortunate autocratic manner meant that his influence was limited to the South East and caused existing British bishops to reject his authority.

St Cuthbert became abbot of the monastery at Lindisfarne, having originally been a shepherd on the Scottish borders. Cuthbert did much to spread Christianity throughout north-east England in the 7th century. The historian Bede called him a 'Child of God'.

Bede too is venerated for his lifetime of devoted scholarship at Jarrow. His seminal work, *The Ecclesiastical History of the English People*, provides a vivid insight into life in the 8th century. St Boniface considered him 'a candle of the church, lit by the Holy Spirit'.

Today, the tombs of both saints lie in the glorious Norman cathedral at Durham, dedicated to Christ, Blessed Mary the Virgin and St Cuthbert.

LEFT: St Augustine of Canterbury, who died in England c.604, less than a decade after landing in Kent. Detail from a window at Beverley Minster.

ABOVE: St Cuthbert's pectoral cross, a superb example of Saxon craftsmanship. Originally buried with him, it is now exhibited in Durham Cathedral.

RIGHT: St Bede, an image from Bede's World, Jarrow, by Peter Murphy.

BELOW: St Aidan, a sculpture by Kathleen Parbury at Lindisfarne Priory. While tending to his flock of sheep, a youthful Cuthbert had a vision of angels conducting St Aidan to heaven. This experience inspired Cuthbert to become a monk.

St Chad

Chad, taught by Aidan at Lindisfarne, succeeded his brother Cedd (who was also canonized) as an abbot. He later became a revered Bishop of Lichfield who insisted in travelling everywhere on foot to preach and, according to Bede, 'administered his diocese in great holiness of life'. Chad died of plague at Lichfield in AD 672.

Reverence and Tears

ABOVE: St Dunstan, Abbot of Glastonbury 940–56, was later Archbishop of Canterbury. He allegedly once healed a dying baby with a kiss. Such miracles came to be seen as proof of sainthood. Today the Vatican requires two miracles prior to canonization.

Many of the early saints were not only greatly revered, but much loved in their local communities, their deaths causing great sorrow.

'They weep today in Salisbury, for he is dead who was the sword of justice and father of Salisbury's church': this was the desolate tribute to St Osmund who founded a cathedral at Old Sarum high on a hill above the city of today, and whose relics are now placed in the present cathedral.

Similarly loved, St Dunstan became Archbishop of Canterbury having been a much respected advisor to successive kings of Wessex. He founded and refounded many abbeys including Glastonbury, Malmesbury, Westminster, Bath and Exeter. Dunstan was a fine musician who played the harp and had such a good voice that a contemporary remarked that when he sang at the altar 'he seemed to be speaking face to face with the Lord'.

Many early saints were of royal descent. St Etheldreda, daughter of a king of the East Angles, married twice, yet neither marriage was consummated. Etheldreda became a nun and later founded a religious house on the Isle of Ely, where the present Ely Cathedral now stands. The many churches dedicated to St Etheldreda indicate how much she was revered throughout Anglo-Saxon England.

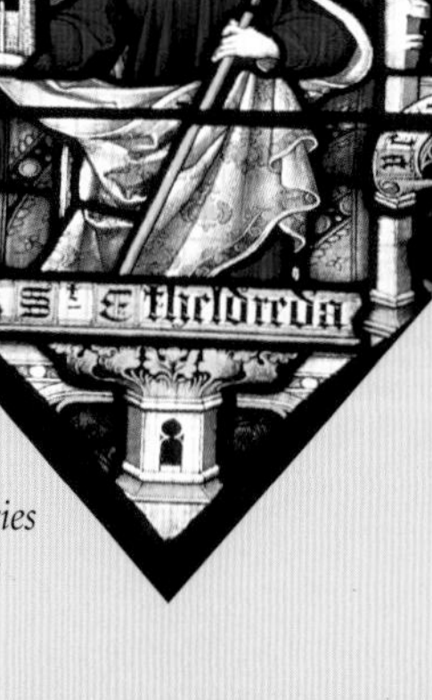

RIGHT: This image of St Etheldreda is near the chapel dedicated to her at Ely Cathedral, which contains a fine modern sculpture of the saint. Her story is told in a series of 14th-century carvings on the sides of arches around the cathedral's octagon.

BOVE: A 20th-century embroidery of St Edmund's brutal xecution at the hands of the Danes, from St Edmundsbury Cathedral at Bury St Edmunds.

Another 'royal saint' from East Anglia was King Edmund. In 869, after ruling peacefully for everal years, he was captured by Danish invaders. Their leader, Ingwar, demanded that Edmund renounce his faith and pay homage to him. For his refusal to yield, the king was tied to a ree and riddled with arrows before being beheaded. Edmund was quickly acknowledged as a saint and his body was later enshrined at Bury St Edmunds, the location of the present-day St Edmundsbury Cathedral.

Edward the Confessor, too, was an English saint-king. Not the most dynamic of English rulers, he was nevertheless a pious, kindly and generous man for whom the term 'saintly' is particularly apt.

The epithet 'confessor' acknowledges that he bore witness to Christ by his exemplary life. Edward's medieval shrine remains intact behind the high altar of the church he built, Westminster Abbey.

The Legend of St Swithun

St Swithun's day, if ye do rain,
For forty days it will remain;
St Swithun's day an ye be fair,
For forty days 'twill rain nae mair.

Before his death ten years later, St Swithun, Bishop of Winchester from 852, requested to be buried humbly in the churchyard, so that 'the sweet rain of heaven might fall upon his grave'. The legend goes that when the authorities attempted to move his remains to a golden shrine inside the cathedral a series of violent storms ensued.

An Archbishop Dies, a Saint is Born

In 1162, Henry II appointed Thomas Becket, his Chancellor and close friend, to be Archbishop of Canterbury. For Henry, this proved to be a grave error. Before long, his loyal, fun-loving, brilliant Chancellor had metamorphosed into an austere, confrontational man of God who with ferocious zeal championed the Church against the Crown, to the delight of the Pope and the fury of the king.

Henry's ire soon caused Becket to flee to France, and it was six years before their quarrel was patched up. The archbishop, returned in triumph to Canterbury. Unshaken in his resolve to assert the Church's rights, Thomas was already prepared for martyrdom: 'I am come to die among you,' he declared. 'In the church there are martyrs and God will soon increase their number.'

Faced with Becket's excommunication of his tame bishops, the king, incandescent with rage, supposedly uttered the infamous and fateful words 'Will no one rid me of this turbulent priest?'. Four eager-to-please knights, Reginald Fitz Urse, William de Tracy, Richard Brito and Hugh de Morville, immediately sailed for England to seek out Becket. On 29 December 1170, they broke into the Archbishop's

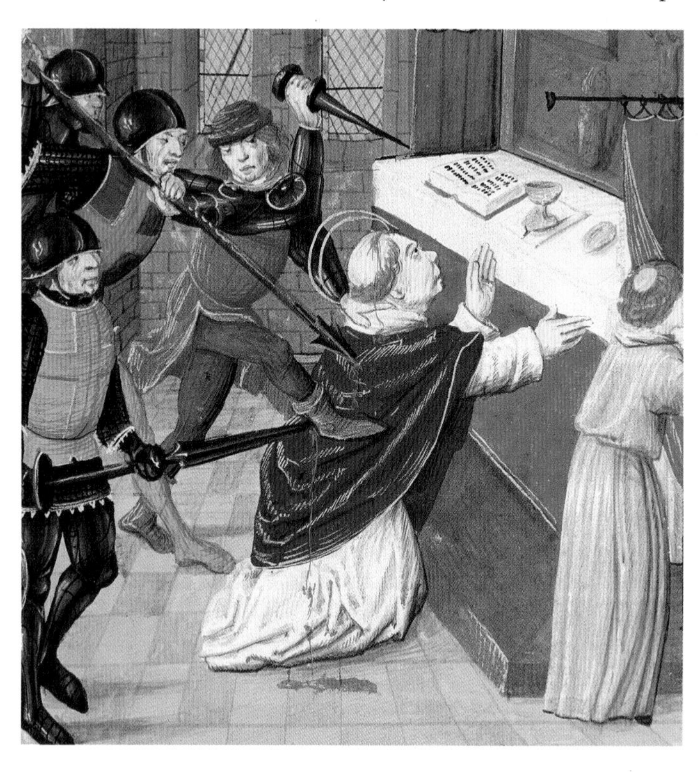

ABOVE: 'For the name of Jesus and protection of the Church, I am ready to embrace death,' prayed Becket as the knights attacked him.

'Will no one rid me of this turbulent priest?'
Henry II referring to Thomas Becket,
in the hearing of his knights

ABOVE: This modern memorial and a bare stone altar mark the scene of Becket's murder.

Palace and confronted him, pursuing him in the twilight into the cathedral, where Vespers was being held. An eyewitness, Edward Grim, gave a graphic account of the ensuing events. As worshippers fled in panic, Becket faced the drawn swords of the four knights calmly in the north-west transept, declaring, 'Lo! Here I am, no traitor to the king, but a priest. What do you seek from me?' Terrified monks tried to drag the archbishop to safety, but the vengeful knights in an unspeakable frenzy of violence hacked him down with a series of blows.

The atrocity of Becket's murder shocked the whole of Christendom, an impact so profound that the king felt compelled to undergo a humiliating period of public penance. Stripped to the waist, he walked barefoot through the streets of Canterbury to kneel at Becket's tomb, to spend long hours in silent vigil scourged by monks.

Becket's impressive shrine attracted pilgrims from all over Europe, inspiring Geoffrey Chaucer to write *The Canterbury Tales*. The four knights were banished to the Holy Land to atone for their sins. An archbishop was dead; the nation's best known martyr had been born.

LEFT: St Thomas Becket, robed and mitred as the archbishop, in a 13th-century panel from the Trinity Chapel at Canterbury Cathedral.

From Strife to Sainthood

Henry II's clash with Thomas Becket was by no means an isolated incident. During the Middle Ages, Church and Crown were often in conflict. Both Henry and his son Richard I were in dispute with the great Bishop (later Saint) Hugh of Lincoln who, soon after his enthronement in 1181, excommunicated royal foresters and refused to give Henry's courtiers church preferments. Hugh soothed him by cracking an impudent joke and, having refused in 1197 to provide men or money towards Richard's overseas campaigns, disarmed him with a kiss.

When Hugh died in 1200, a monk wrote of 'his great compassion and tenderness towards the sick, and even to those afflicted with leprosy. He used to wash and dry their feet and kiss them affectionately, and having refreshed them with food and drink, gave them alms on a lavish scale'.

A rather more curious Lincoln saint was Little St Hugh, a 9-year-old boy whose corpse was

The west front of Lincoln Cathedral. St Hugh of Lincoln, the man central to its Gothic re-creation, is the figure on the south-west (right) pinnacle.

ABOVE: *St Richard of Chichester, a statue located by his shrine in Chichester Cathedral*

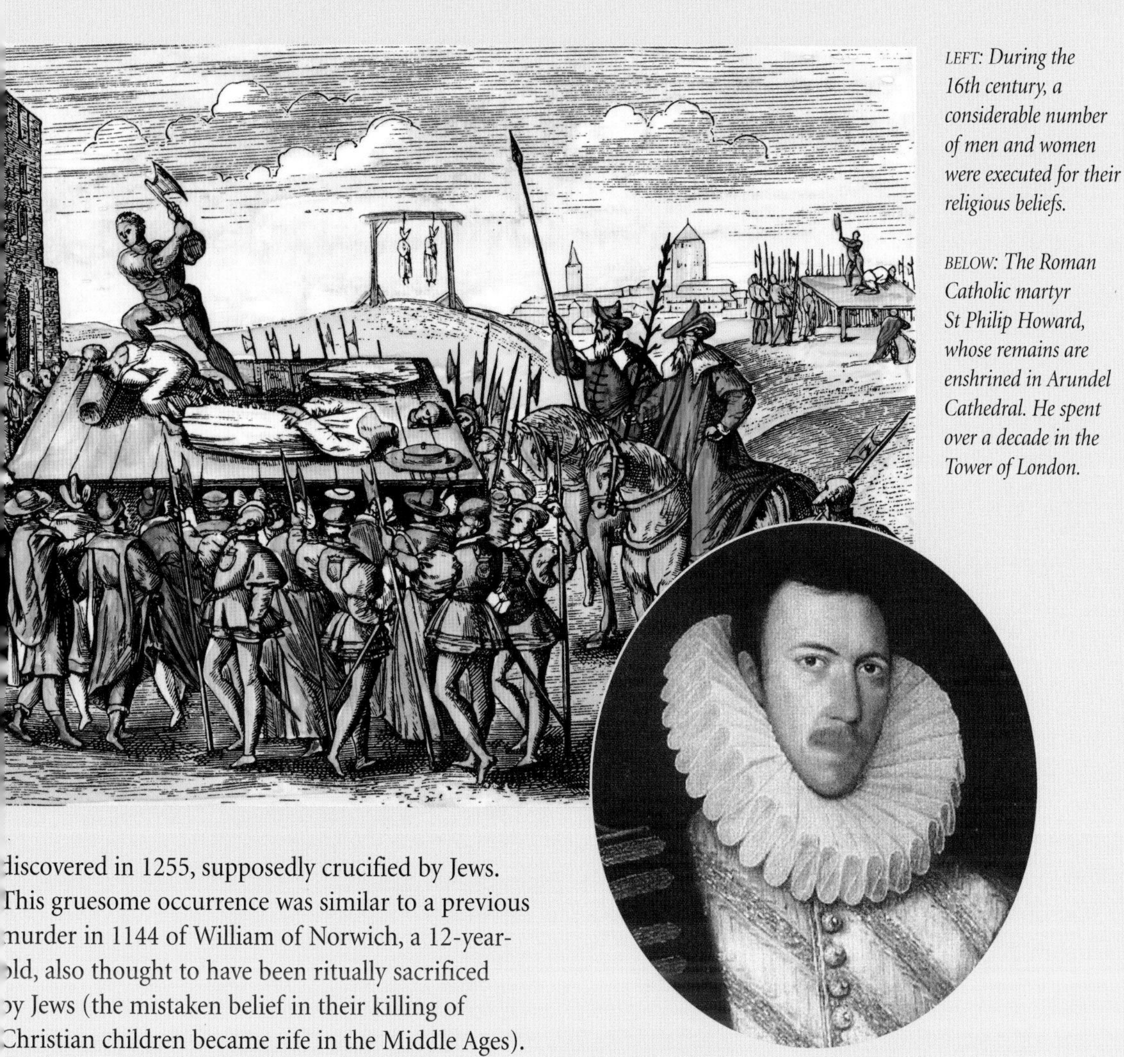

LEFT: During the 16th century, a considerable number of men and women were executed for their religious beliefs.

BELOW: The Roman Catholic martyr St Philip Howard, whose remains are enshrined in Arundel Cathedral. He spent over a decade in the Tower of London.

discovered in 1255, supposedly crucified by Jews. This gruesome occurrence was similar to a previous murder in 1144 of William of Norwich, a 12-year-old, also thought to have been ritually sacrificed by Jews (the mistaken belief in their killing of Christian children became rife in the Middle Ages). Anti-Semitism led to Edward I expelling the Jews from England in the late 13th century.

Henry III had opposed Richard of Wych's appointment as Bishop of Chichester, wanting his own man, Robert Passelewe. A two-year feud resulted, leaving Richard without his episcopal estates or home. Eventually Henry caved in under threat of excommunication, while Richard's sanctity and pastoral devotion vindicated his appointment and led to his canonization in 1262.

The conflicts created by the Reformation, the Protestant religious revolution which swept across Western Europe during the 16th century, inevitably created further martyrs and saints. Thomas More, Henry VIII's Lord Chancellor, and John Fisher, Bishop of Rochester, both opposed the king becoming head of the Church of England, and were executed in 1535. Although in poor health, the elderly Fisher survived imprisonment in the Tower of London and met his death bravely. When the Pope made him a cardinal, the king declared that by the time Fisher received the red hat, he would no longer have a head to put it on. Both More and Fisher were canonized in 1935.

Robert Southwell, Edmund Campion and Thomas Garnet were 16th-century Jesuits, religious fanatics coming to England fully prepared, even eager, for martyrdom. When captured, they were tortured then hanged, drawn and quartered. Philip Howard, Earl of Arundel, was also imprisoned in the Tower, where he died, aged 38, in 1595, possibly from poison. Howard and the Jesuits were some of 40 Roman Catholic martyrs who sacrificed themselves for their faith during the Reformation and were canonized in 1970, the last in a long line of English saints.

Thomas More: the Making of a Martyr

Henry VIII's Lord Chancellor, the 'Man for All Seasons' of Robert Bolt's famous film, was full of contradictions. Beneath his magnificent chain and robes of office Thomas More, as Becket had done, wore the hair shirt, a deliberately uncomfortable garment worn as a penance by many medieval ascetics. A former lawyer and an intellectual, More could appear solemn and serious in public, dismissive of the dim-witted aristocracy. In private, though, he was witty, warm-hearted and a loving family man. A close friend of Erasmus, whose writing greatly influenced the Reformation, More was nevertheless immensely intolerant of Protestantism, the new cutting edge of Christianity. He was deeply dismayed when in 1533 the king decided to divorce his first wife, Catherine of Aragon, to marry Anne Boleyn and utterly horrified when Henry began proceedings to make himself head of the Church of England.

In protest at royal interference in spiritual affairs, More resigned the chancellorship and returned to private life. In 1534 Henry introduced the Act of Supremacy, pronouncing himself as head of the Church. The Act required all his adult subjects to submit to an oath of allegiance. More's refusal to take the oath represented a deafening silence from such a high-profile figure.

Infuriated, Henry sent him to the Tower of London. More remained as a prisoner in the Bell Tower for over a year, while the king hoped he might change his mind and take the oath. More did not. He was deeply religious and obeyed his conscience as if it were the word of God, regardless of the consequences.

Tried for high treason at the Palace of Westminster, More, with his legal background, produced a skilful defence, but to no avail. The judges, under severe pressure from Henry, found him guilty and sentenced him to death. In the summer of 1535, More faced his executioner on Tower Hill, declaring that he died 'the king's good servant but God's first'. The axe fell, and another martyr was created.

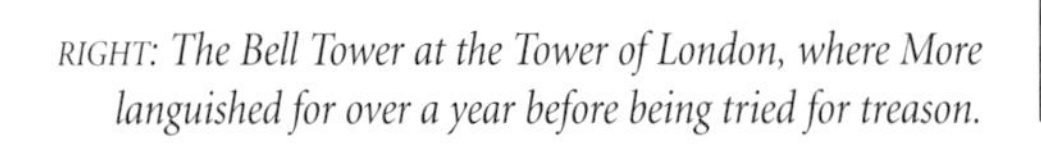

RIGHT: The Bell Tower at the Tower of London, where More languished for over a year before being tried for treason.

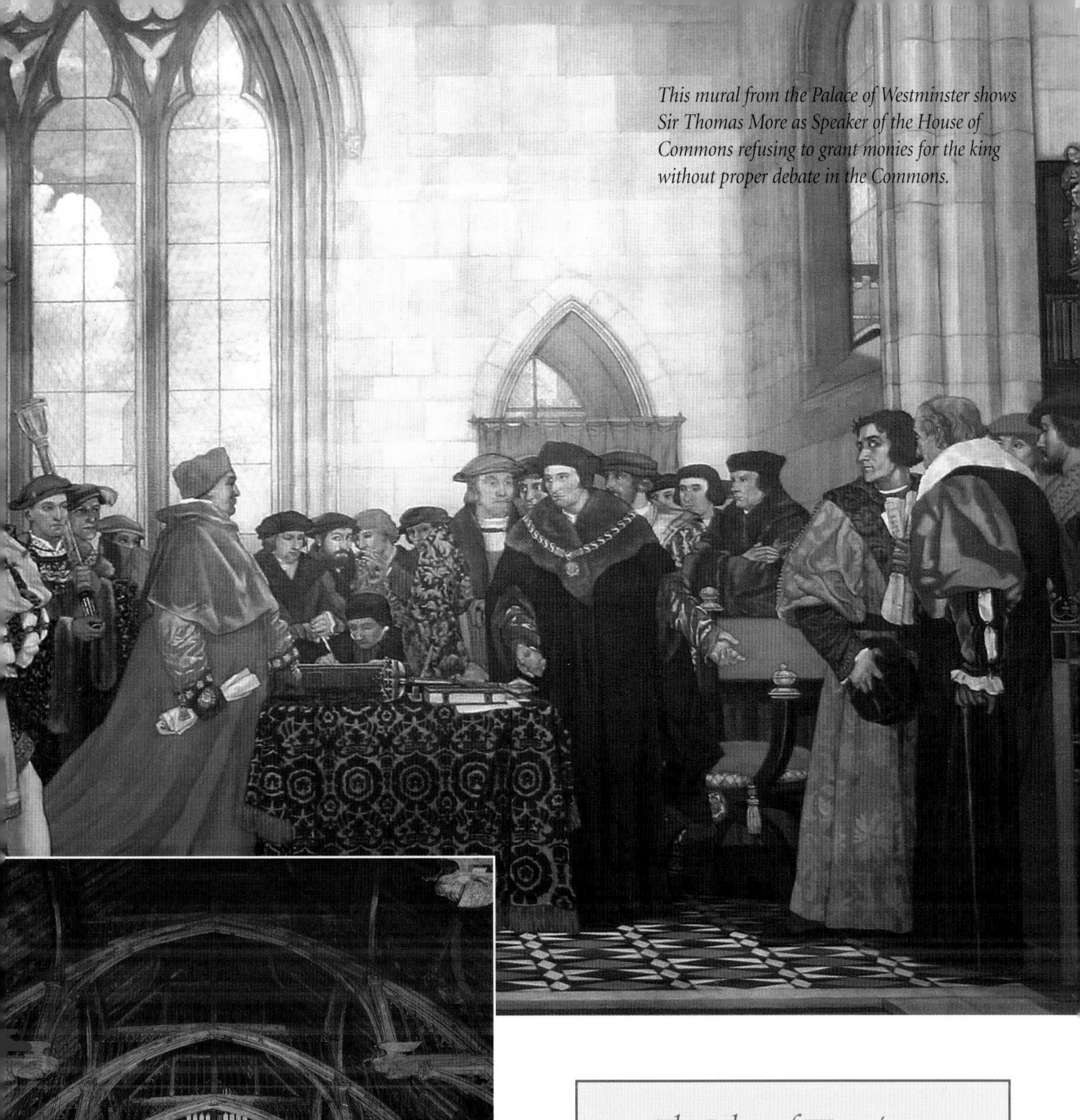

This mural from the Palace of Westminster shows Sir Thomas More as Speaker of the House of Commons refusing to grant monies for the king without proper debate in the Commons.

BOVE: Westminster Hall was the scene of the dramatic treason trials f Sir Thomas More, Charles I and Guy Fawkes.

The Palace of Westminster

Saints are well represented within the Palace of Westminster. There is a mural of Sir Thomas More in St Stephen's Hall and in the Central Lobby, a mosaic of St George by Sir Edward Poynter, the mid 19th-century President of the Royal Acadamy. A statue of St George can be found in the Robing Room of the House of Lords, murals of St Edmund and St Etheldreda feature in the undercroft chapel, whilst the Norman Porch leading to the Royal Staircase contains a stained-glass window depicting Edward the Confessor.

A Sense of Awe and Wonder

The adoration of saints has resulted in artistry and craftsmanship of the highest order. Stained glass, statuary, wall paintings, carvings in wood and stone are by no means confined to the great cathedrals, but can also be discovered in churches throughout the nation. For example, St Mary's at Fairford in Gloucestershire and St Neots in Cornwall contain the most complete medieval glass to be found anywhere in England, much of it depicting saints. The stained glass of the Pre-Raphaelites, created in the late 19th century by William Morris and Edward Burne-Jones, can be seen in many English churches. St Martin's at Scarborough in Yorkshire is particularly notable, the imagery of saints simply sublime.

ABOVE: The reredos at Chester Cathedral shows Oswald, King of Northumbria, praying with his soldiers before battle. He established Christianity in his kingdom before being martyred and becoming a saint.

RIGHT: A 15th-century window in a bay of the south choir aisle at York Minster features the life of St Cuthbert. Superb medieval glass is one of the highlights of the Minster.

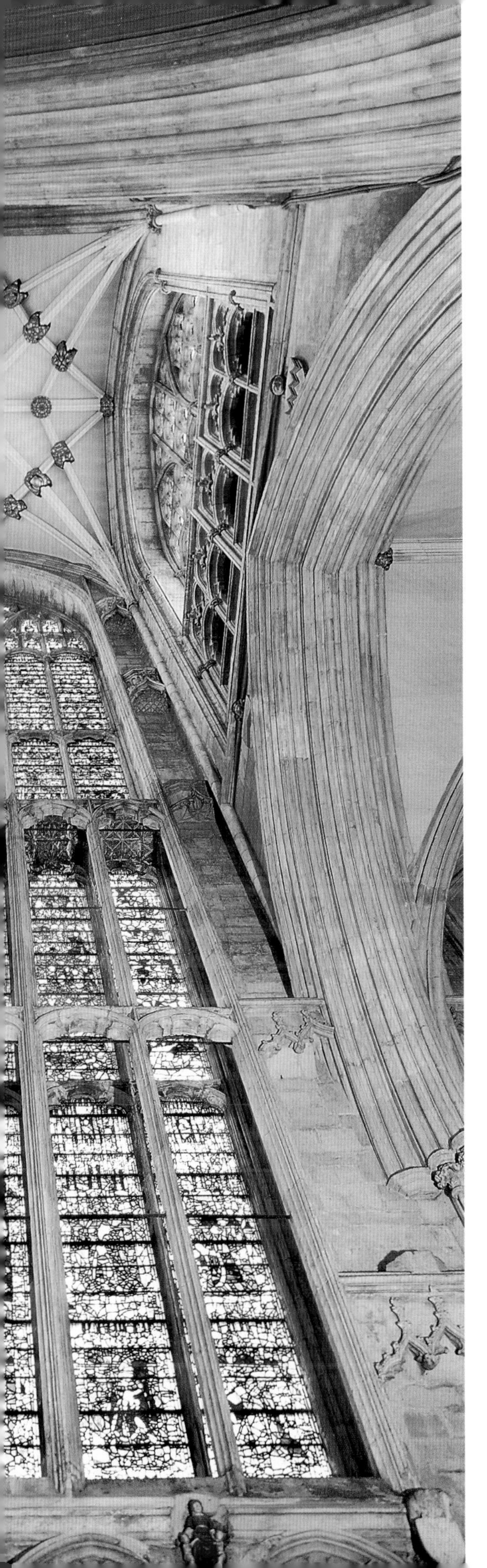

ABOVE: A carving of St Werburgh (1993) by Joseph Pyrz in Chester Cathedral. Werburgh inspired the foundation of the Benedictine abbey in the city.

Iconography – the use of pictures or symbols in the visual arts – also flourished in medieval cathedrals, from Durham, York and Lincoln in the north to Westminster, Salisbury and Winchester in the south; from Norwich and Canterbury in the east to Exeter and Wells in the West Country. In these places are pieces of outstanding merit, all the more remarkable when one considers the limited technology of the time. Sculptors, painters, carpenters, glaziers and other highly-skilled craftsmen worked in close harmony to achieve creativity of exquisite ecclesiastical beauty, symbolizing man's enduring faith and his love of God.

This sacred art and architecture was intended to produce a sense of awe and wonderment, almost of theatre, both in local worshippers and in the thousands of pilgrims who flocked from afar, many of whom could neither read nor write. Here, in accessible form, was God Almighty, Christ in Majesty, angels and archangels, together with the saints – the Heavenly Host. Thus images of saints appeared in rich, vibrant colours on stained glass and murals, together with statues and bas reliefs, carved in wood or stone or fashioned in metal.

Stained Glass and Iconography

ABOVE: *St Frideswide, Oxford's patron saint, depicted by Edward Burne-Jones in Christ Church Cathedral, Oxford.*

BELOW: *Statues of saints on Salisbury Cathedral's west front. They are (from left to right): St Barbara, St Catherine, St Roche, St Nicholas, St George, St Christopher, St Sebastian, St Cogmas, St Damian, St Margaret and St Ursula.*

The Reformation was a watershed for Englis religion. The fact that saints were now viewed from a different perspective brough catastrophic consequences for decorative features i many of the nation's churches and cathedrals.

The Protestant emphasis was on simplicity of worship. Invoking the saints has never been part of Anglican liturgy and 16th-century Protestant extremists regarded church ornamentation as papist. Thus a large amount of medieval artistry and craftsmanship was wantonly destroyed by Tudor iconoclasts in pursuit of theological correctness. Many niches once occupied by stone saints now lie empty. At Salisbury Cathedral in the 17th century, Oliver Cromwell's Puritan soldiers ar said to have used the statues of saints above the we door as targets for musket practice. These have onl been restored in the last few years.

Fortunately many saints did survive in glass, stone or wood. Also, a mid 19th-century High Church resurgence together with the Victorians' renewed interest in Gothic forms, added richness and impetus to religious decoration. In addition to the Pre-Raphaelites, George Gilbert Scott, William Butterfield, G.F. Bodley, William Burges and A.W.N. Pugin all provided huge creative input for this welcome burst of sacred art and architecture.

ABOVE: *St Dunstan's Chapel in St Paul's Cathedral, dedicated in 1905. One story has the saint seizing the Devil's nose with a pair of pliers.*

ABOVE: *Niches at Durham Cathedral once held statues of saints and angels which were destroyed during the Reformation.*

In 1872 it was Queen Victoria herself who prompted decorative additions to St Paul's Cathedral, Wren's mighty but until then somewhat austere masterpiece. Subsequent introductions were two chapels, one dedicated to St Dunstan, another to St Michael and St George. It was also during this era that the neo-Gothic Truro Cathedral was built and dedicated to St Mary, the first entirely new foundation since the Reformation.

For many centuries England's cathedrals and churches have continued to be showpieces of artistic genius, exceptional human creativity inspired by the transcendent superhuman qualities – heroism, piety, sacrifice – of the saints.

Shrines and Pilgrimages

In the Middle Ages, pilgrims flocked in their thousands to shrines: places with saintly connections. Perhaps they sought penance for a wrongdoing, perhaps the fulfilment of a prayer, perhaps even a miraculous cure for an affliction.

A shrine usually was a casket of wood, stone or metal, containing sacred relics, but it can also be an altar, tomb or chapel associated with a saint. Historically, pilgrimages were a mixture of piety and pleasure: part religious devotion, part holiday excursion, brilliantly portrayed in Chaucer's late 14th-century pilgrim saga.

Pilgrims were big business, and relics sometimes emerged in questionable circumstances. In the 9th century, the supposed remains of St James were fortuitously unearthed near a small village in a remote part of north-west Spain. Despite there being no evidence that the relics belong to James, today he is Spain's patron saint and Santiago de Compostela one of the most popular pilgrimage destinations in Western Europe.

It happened in medieval England too. In 1184 at Glastonbury, fire consumed the great Norman monastery there. Funds to rebuild it were insufficient; King Richard was away fighting a costly war in the Holy Land. But, in 1191, monks discovered the grave of King Arthur and Queen Guinevere within the abbey grounds. Hordes of pilgrims flocked to see it, money flowed in and a magnificent new abbey was the result.

Numerous wonderful shrines met a sad end during Henry VIII's Dissolution of the Monasteries in the 16th century. Most famous of these was that of Thomas Becket at Canterbury, where 26 wagons were needed to carry off the spoils. Among many other saints to suffer similarly were St Alban, St Wulfstan (Worcester), St Werburgh (Chester) and St Hugh (Lincoln). Today, pilgrims still visit Canterbury and the many other sacred places to be found in England.

Our Lady of Walsingham

Late in the 11th century, Richeldis de Faverches, a widowed Norfolk noblewoman, had a vision in which she was transported to the Virgin Mary's home at Nazareth. Richeldis was instructed to replicate this as a place of healing and her village, Walsingham, became known as The English Nazareth. Many miracles occurred there. The shrine was destroyed by Henry VIII in 1538 but restored in the early 20th century, today attracting many thousands of pilgrims. Anglican, Methodist, Roman Catholic and Russian Orthodox faiths are all represented in the village.

ABOVE: *The shrine of St Edward the Confessor survived the Reforma... can be found behind the High Altar at Westminster Abbey.*